How to Get
APPOINTMENTS
Without Rejection

Fill Our Calendars with
Network Marketing
Prospects

KEITH & TOM "BIG AL" SCHREITER

How to Get Appointments Without Rejection

© 2020 by Keith & Tom "Big Al" Schreiter

Published by Fortune Network Publishing

PO Box 890084

Houston, TX 77289 USA

Telephone: +1 (281) 280-9800

BigAlBooks.com

ISBN-13: 978-1-948197-71-7

Contents

Preface

"My phone feels like it weighs 500 pounds. I will do anything rather than call for an appointment."

As network marketers, we hear this all the time. Why? Because it is true. The fear of calling for an appointment overwhelms even our best intentions. We can set goals, jump up and down enthusiastically, and chant affirmations in front of our mirrors. Nothing seems to work. Why?

Because as network marketers, we have common sense. We try to get appointments, fail, get rejected, and learn a lesson. The lesson is this: "Don't continue ruining our self-image with humiliating attempts to get appointments."

Why is getting appointments so difficult?

Is it our mindset? Do we lack the skill of knowing exactly what to say?

In most cases, the answer is "Yes" to both questions.

Let's fix these two problems now. Then we can fly forward in our network marketing careers.

"Why are you talking funny?"

Let's say we call up our good friend, John.

Us: "Hello, John? I am calling to see when would be a good time for us to chat."

John thinks, "Huh? Why is my friend talking so funny? It doesn't sound like my friend. Did an alien take over his body? I don't feel comfortable with this strange tone of voice."

John: "What is this all about?"

Us: "Oh, it will only take 20 minutes. I want to show you something amazing and exciting. When is a good time?"

John thinks, "I have hundreds of things to do. Decisions to make. Places to go. I don't even have 20 seconds. But this is my friend. What can I say to put this off? I don't have time to waste. Let me find out if this will be something I am not interested in. I have to stop this from going further."

John: "So tell me a little bit about this first. Can you give me a few details?"

Us: "Not really. It is visual. I am not selling anything. Trust me. You have to see it in person. When do you have 20 minutes for a cup of coffee?"

What is John thinking now? "This sounds like a salesman." Now John becomes very skeptical. Time to put this off forever without offending us.

John: "Is this something I have to eat or sample, or is it something to look at?"

Us: "I have this presentation I want you to look at."

John's brain reacts. "Presentation? I know that word. Salesman approaching! Run! Run! Save myself. Hide my wallet! Lock the doors!"

John: "Uh … sounds interesting, I guess. But I don't have time this week. Let me get back to you when I have some free time. I've got to run right now and rearrange my bottle cap collection."

Getting appointments can be brutal.

This is unfair.

New team members don't have a chance. They are amateurs.

Let's imagine John again. He has a change of heart and joins our business tonight. By paying to join our business, do we gift John with:

- Unlimited confidence?
- Professional sales skills?
- Total product and compensation plan mastery?
- A list of common objections and their answers?
- Instant self-esteem?
- A courage transplant?
- A script containing exactly what to say for appointments?

No. John is an amateur.

What is the first thing we ask John to do? Call his friends and attempt to get appointments!

A bad ending is coming. Why?

Because John's friends are professionals. Their entire lives have been spent practicing how to reject salespeople and sales appointment approaches. With years of building skills to avoid appointments, they are ready.

Seems like we're sending John into an unfair situation, and it won't end well for him.

Let's give John a chance and give him the tools to succeed in getting appointments.

17 networkers attempted this, and failed.

17 networkers attempted to get an appointment with my evil uncle. It was a massacre. The remaining networkers had the common sense to not even try.

Okay, a slight exaggeration, but we know how hard it is to get appointments. Here are a few reasons we don't even try:

- Prospects are sales-resistant. Everyone is pitching them. **Everyone.**
- We have common sense and hate rejection.
- We don't like asking for our prospects' time.
- Our desire for comfort is greater than our desire for money.

So what do evil uncles say?

- "Tell me what scheme you are pitching now, Pyramid Boy!"
- "Stop dreaming. Be normal like the rest of us."
- "I can't believe you think I would want to pester my friends."
- "I don't care what it is. I am not interested."
- "Give up. These things never work out."
- "I don't have time ... for anything!"

Scary.

Cold prospects can be worse. Why don't we call or reach out more?

Is it a lack of motivation? No. We have motivation. We have goals and dreams.

Then what is holding us back? What is holding our teams back?

Let's discover the two reasons getting appointments feels so hard.

Thinking in circles won't fix our appointment problem.

We worry. We want to succeed. And yet, we don't attempt to get appointments.

The result? Guilt.

It is easy to let our fear and anxiety accumulate. Every day we don't set or even attempt to set appointments, our spirits are crushed a little more. Our minds go in circles looking for solutions. We ask ourselves, "Should I try harder? What am I missing? What is wrong with me? Am I scared? Why am I failing?"

This is not productive. Using up our brain power on random questions won't help us to fix this problem.

What should we be asking ourselves instead?

Am I not setting appointments because:

1. I **won't** do it?

2. I **can't** do it?

"I won't do it."

Yes. This is a mindset problem, a huge obstacle. Getting our heads right, fixing our internal stories, and relieving our fears can be daunting. Fortunately, we will learn how to fix these things in the chapters ahead.

The biggest challenge we have is the "I won't do it" problem. If we never start, our chances are zero. If we solve the "I won't do it" problem, we are 90% of the way to unlimited appointments.

"I can't do it."

This is the easier problem to fix. Learning rejection-free skills will be quick and efficient.

When we start network marketing, we don't know the scripts and the "what to do" skills. We don't understand the subconscious programs in our prospects' minds. But we can learn. We learned how to use a smartphone. We learned how to drive. We can certainly learn the proper words to fill our calendars with appointments.

We will learn the words to say, we will learn what our prospects expect from us, and we will fix our "head problems" that hold us back.

If we don't get a grip on this problem, our entire group gets infected. We can scare our group by saying, "Let's get on the telephone and start making appointments for presentations." This is cruel. Watch the blood leave their faces. It is like someone sucks the oxygen from their lungs. And it gets worse.

Even if our group makes some calls, a prospect could say, "Tell me what it is all about first." Now our new team members are not only scared, but panicked.

This is a difficult question for new team members. What can they say?

If they say too little, it will look like they are hiding their agenda. Say too much, and the prospects feel like they know everything, and will refuse to set appointments.

So many problems.

Let's start now. First we will address that 600-pound gorilla in the room that messes with our heads: The "I won't do it" problem.

"I won't do it."

Network marketing leader, Nam Do, is the epitome of will-power on steroids. He is fearless, focused, and willing to do whatever it takes to get the job done. Unfortunately, few of us have that kind of discipline.

This chapter is for the rest of us.

Because of fear, many network marketers take this approach to getting appointments:

"I am aggressively waiting for my phone to ring!"

Yeah. Even with a positive attitude, that is not going to work. We have to be more proactive.

When summoning the courage to call prospects for an appointment, there are some objections and feelings that may keep us from moving forward.

We:

- Feel scared.
- Don't want to risk rejection.
- Don't want our friends to think we are trying to make money off them.
- Feel guilty asking our friends for favors.
- Don't know what to say.
- Want to procrastinate.
- Look for ways to avoid this.

- Pretend to do other things that make us look busy.
- Feel guilty because we don't ask for appointments.
- Create graphs and charts of what would happen if we had the courage to do this.

And the list goes on and on.

The forces of resistance overwhelm us. We don't try for appointments. Instead, we rearrange some names on our calendar and watch television.

Why do we procrastinate?

The two main causes of procrastination are:

#1. The task is too large. We did not break the task down into tiny, easy-to-handle steps.

#2. We don't have the skills to perform the task within our comfort zone.

Here are some quick fixes.

#1. The task is too large.

Where do I start? How many people should I call? Who do I call first? Maybe I should work on my responses to objections first? Our internal dialogue wins.

The solution is to make the first step specific and very small. Our minds will say, "Okay, I can do that little bit." Some examples?

- Today I will make a list of the 10 most comfortable people to call.

- Tomorrow, when I return from work, I will call these two people on my list.
- I will call to say "hi" to my friend, and if my friend asks me what is new, I will tell her we should meet for coffee. If she doesn't ask, that is okay.
- I will say to one person today, "If a little extra money every week sounds good to you, let's talk."
- Tomorrow morning, I will text this request for an appointment to two more friends.

Tiny steps. Nothing to fear. Easy to do. Almost effortless.

Procrastination's power crumbles when the first step is easy. Resistance melts away.

If our procrastination still holds power over us, then make our first specific step even smaller!

What about the second cause of procrastination?

#2. We don't have the skills to perform the task within our comfort zone.

This is a real problem. If we only read books, and never practice what we're reading, we procrastinate. We know we don't have the skills.

Here are some examples of skills we might lack that hold us back from making our first call for an appointment.

- What should I say if I get their voicemail?
- If the prospect asks me what it is all about, where do I start?
- What if my prospects ask, "Are you trying to sell me something?"

- What should I say to get them to commit to an appointment?

- When prospects are skeptical, what should I do?

- The prospect says, "Never call me again!" Then what?

We will learn these answers in upcoming chapters. Relax. Don't let fear grasp us by the throat. The words and phrases we will learn will be completely safe, polite, and rejection-free.

"Why do I feel embarrassed?"

The "I won't do it" problem has many sources.

But if we overcome our personal embarrassment, procrastination suffers an instant defeat.

Why do we feel embarrassed when attempting to get appointments?

- We aren't convinced that our offer gives enough value.
- We worry about what others think of our intentions.
- Our internal story predicts defeat before we start.

When we remove personal embarrassment, things get easy. Here is something to think about.

Let's take a yellow personality. Not familiar with the color personalities? Here are the general traits of yellow personalities.

Yellow personalities love to help people. They think about helping others more than they think of their personal needs. They are kind, giving, full of empathy, and they never want to offend or make others uncomfortable. Typical professions where you'll find yellow personalities are kindergarten school teachers, massage therapists, social workers, and charity organizers. They are shy, not pushy, and don't often enter sales professions. And they get their feelings hurt all the time.

Okay, an oversimplification for sure, but we need to make a point.

Ask a yellow personality to call for appointments and sell a product. Instant resistance.

Ask a yellow personality to call for appointments to get people to donate to a worthy cause. Instant engagement. They are fearless. They never get tired. Never get discouraged. Never get embarrassed when asking for donations.

Do we see the difference?

Embarrassment melts away when our internal story reflects belief in what we do.

Yellow personalities can overcome their fears immediately to raise funds and make cold calls. Their courage has nothing to do with the commission and bonus plan, a car program, qualifying for a holiday, or ranking up to get recognition for a promotion.

Let this sink into our minds.

Ordinary reward motivation doesn't work as well as belief.

Change our internal story and we can change our lives.

Prospects react to our internal story.

If we don't create a story for our minds, someone else will. We don't want some random story by others to get inside of our minds. That's not good.

Paul Smith wrote the book, *Sell With A Story*. He describes an experiment. We modified the experiment explanation to show a network marketing analogy for us.

Salespeople, group #1. This group received no new internal story. In the next two weeks, their sales were consistent.

Salespeople, group #2. This group received an internal story of how awesome their careers will be as they succeed. They heard about the cars, the bonuses, and the promotions. Their sales were also consistent over the two-week period.

Huh? No change? But wouldn't this new internal story motivate the salespeople? In this case, no. The sales were the same.

We might rethink telling our team members to set more goals or to improve the pictures on their vision board. Just a thought. If the reward is only for them, it doesn't seem to help their internal belief levels.

Salespeople, group #3. They received an internal story of how previous customers benefited from and enjoyed what was sold. For our network marketing example here, group #3 heard testimonials of satisfied customers.

This group doubled their sales over the two-week period.

Doubled? What???

Yes.

How could this be? Could it be that we are less afraid of talking to others when we are not worried about our own personal gain?

What if our new agenda was solely to help others? Would that help us overcome our embarrassment and reluctance to call for appointments?

Yes.

Remember those fearless yellow personalities.

Don't use conscious willpower to fight personal embarrassment. Instead, take the easier option of changing our internal story.

The big point? Each of the three groups had their own stories inside their heads. This story affected their results. The good news is that we can change our internal story at any time, at no cost.

And what happens when we do this?

Our prospects become more open when we call for appointments. Prospects are reactive. They respond not only to the words we say, but their feelings about our agenda.

This case study is disturbing.

In network marketing, we say, "Personal development makes the difference."

We set goals, create vision boards, chant affirmations, sing the company song, read inspirational books, go to power-packed motivational events, and believe this will make a difference in our internal motivation and effectiveness.

But remember the case study. We gave group #2 a vision of how their lives could improve. Yet, their results remained the same.

Remember group #3? We showed them how their product or service helped others. Their results doubled. By thinking of the benefit to others, their courage and conviction increased. Prospects noticed the difference and bought or joined.

What could this mean to us if we are trying to resurrect an inactive team member? Or if we are trying to build our courage to talk to prospects?

Maybe we should concentrate on the contribution to society by exposing more people to the products and opportunity. When we think less about ourselves, and more about others, there is no room for fear.

Does this go against everything we were taught about personal development? We will let you decide. However, this certainly looks like a good avenue for us to overcome our fear and anxieties about reaching out to others.

What about mental blackmail?

It's temporary at best. And it makes us feel bad.

An example? We set a goal to earn enough for our spouse to retire. And then we don't call to make appointments. We ask ourselves, "Did I change my mind? Is this not important to me anymore?"

Guilt. Terrible feelings. Maybe we try to make a call or two, but we don't enjoy it. This isn't going to work long-term.

Long-term success requires that we change the story inside our heads. Unless we enjoy the process, we will stop. Willpower is not strong enough for us to endure.

How do prospects notice the difference when we change our internal story?

Everyone has a subconscious mind program that scans people we meet for clues. We don't consciously think about all the clues. Our subconscious mind takes care of this for us. In less than a second, it analyzes the clues. Then it tells our conscious mind what the other person's intention or agenda is.

Here is how we got that program. Many thousands of years ago, a caveman went hunting. He met a stranger. Now was that stranger safe, or a potential threat? The cavemen learned what to notice to determine good or bad intentions. If the caveman was wrong, well, that mistake meant he didn't live to reproduce. The surviving cavemen got the intention detection right.

What kinds of clues do we notice? Here are four big ones.

1. Body language. We look for signs of aggression or hidden agendas. Sometimes it is obvious. We see someone come in the door and think, "Why is that person wearing a hockey mask and carrying an axe?" Definitely bad body language.

2. Tone of voice. Even as children, we could sense if Mom was angry or happy by her tone of voice.

3. Micro-facial expressions. Our faces give our intentions away. Our faces can show up to 30 different micro-facial expressions per second. Our subconscious mind knows how to read those micro-facial expressions. When Mom looks inside our room, before she even says a word, we look at her face to see if we are in trouble. (On the positive side, children look at their parents' faces to decide if now is a good time to ask permission for something.)

4. Words. Yes, we judge people harshly by their opening words. Feel how these words affect us:

- Presentation versus option.
- Present versus chat.
- Opportunity versus chance.
- Change versus improvement.
- Meet-up versus meeting.

- Pop by versus visit.

- In the area versus I will come.

- Objection versus problem.

Bottom line?

If we change how we talk to ourselves (our internal story), our prospects notice and react.

How do we change our internal story?

Simple. Start telling ourselves a new story. And if we can't internalize our new story, well, repetition helps.

Wait ... we are telling ourselves a story?

Yes. And our new story will replace the old story we told ourselves. Unfortunately, most of what is in our minds are stories. These stories are the interpretations of what we chose to tell ourselves. An example?

"This glass is half-full."

"This glass is half-empty."

We choose which story we tell ourselves.

We create stories about different political parties, sports teams, fashions, opinions, and our lives. We create stories about what happens to us. We even have stories about who we think we are. Our minds are just big story factories.

We create our own stories.

Let's create a new story about getting appointments. We know our old story. Remember?

- Prospects don't want to be bothered.
- No one answers our calls.
- Prospects think I want to make money off them.

- No one wants to change.
- I hate rejection.
- Prospects are busy. No one has extra time in their days.
- Others will make fun of me.
- Everyone will look at me as a pushy salesperson.
- Appointments are hard.

What could be our new story? How about:

- People want more money in their life.
- This is an opportunity of a lifetime.
- Everyone wants these products.
- I don't have to sell anything. Instead, I give them more choices.
- People want me to solve their problems.
- People hope I can help them.
- Appointments are easy.

When we tell this new story to ourselves, our fear and anxieties go away. How many times do we have to tell ourselves this story? For most of us, many times. But it is worth it.

Getting appointments is less about scripts and personal motivation, and more about relieving our anxiety and fear of reaching out to people.

If we feel guilty, now we know why. It is our internal story.

When fixing problems, we must first correctly identify the core problem.

If we or our team are not making appointments, let's work on the anxiety and fears first.

Here are three tools we can use for these fears and anxieties:

1. Beliefs. (We are changing those with our internal story.)

2. Expectations. (Be realistic. Understand others and have empathy.)

3. Skills. (We will get to these shortly.)

Our fears prevent us from even trying. Here is a story that shows it is easier to "feel" the problem in a story than to explain the problem.

The ice cream story.

I like ice cream. In fact, I love ice cream. And what is better than ice cream? Free ice cream!

Imagine we get unlimited ice cream for life delivered to our home.

What is the catch?

We can eat free ice cream whenever we want. But each time, before we eat, we must stick needles underneath our fingernails.

What???

Sounds painful to me. Plus, I have an aversion to needles. I hate needles! My childhood memories of wood splinters underneath a fingernail make me shiver.

Feel the discomfort? Thinking about the pain? Considering having cake instead of ice cream?

For me, I would go for pie, cake, cookies … anything but ice cream.

I am not alone. Most humans avoid pain. Comfort is our friend.

What is the lesson here?

"No matter how big the reward, if the process or activity that leads to that reward is uncomfortable, humans resist."

Yes, we can mentally force ourselves for a little while. However, if the process or activity is unpleasant, we will eventually stop.

The secret is to make the activity enjoyable.

A catchy script isn't going to solve this problem. This is a mental problem, not a simple word skill.

What about "guru" advice?

Guru advice is technically correct. Logical. Sensible.

And it doesn't work with humans.

Humans are not logical, sensible beings. Our brains are survival organs. Thinking logically and sensibly is fantasy. Here are some examples of good technical advice that don't work with our human wiring.

"Eat less. Exercise more. Lose weight." If that worked, we wouldn't have overweight people in this world. It sounds good, but it is not advice that we can follow as humans. We have other programs that override this good advice. It only takes a casual glance to prove to ourselves that this advice doesn't work.

"Be brave. Face the fear. And the fear will melt away." Well, that was easy for the guru to say, but we are the ones that have to face this fear. And what happens? We face the fear and we are still scared. We don't like it at all. The fear does not melt away. Apparently our fear was not listening to the guru's advice.

"Spend less. Earn more. Then, we will be rich." Those instructions were not hard. Anyone could follow those. Does it happen? Almost never. Only a few outliers can put this advice to work. For most humans, that advice might as well be in a foreign language.

"Want more appointments? Talk to more strangers." Where have we heard this before? Everywhere! And is this what we do? No. As humans, we are more concerned with avoiding rejection, feeling good about ourselves, and not damaging our self-esteem. Those programs are more powerful, so we don't talk to more strangers. Again, great advice, but not followed by humans.

Do we see a pattern here? The rewards for following this advice would be awesome. However, we let our other programs, such as avoiding discomfort, rule what we do. As humans, our internal wiring says, "Avoid pain. Avoid discomfort." In the hierarchy of programs, this is near the top.

The better advice would be, "Find a way to get appointments that is comfortable. If we can stay within our comfort zone, this is something we will do."

What determines our comfort zone?

Our internal story, the story we tell ourselves.

The good news is that we can create a new story any time we want. Every story in our mind is made-up. Why not make up a story that serves us, instead of holds us back?

Options.

"Option" is one of our favorite words.

What does the word "option" mean to prospects? It means that it is okay to say "yes" or "no" to our suggestion. It will only be one more choice in their lives. They can save our option until later. We won't high-pressure them to take our option now. There is no guilt or shame in not acting on the options we offered them.

What does the word "option" mean to us? It means there is no "yes" or "no," live or die, high-pressure in the moment. We simply offer our prospects one more option for their lives. Now it is up to the prospects to decide if that option serves them or not.

No rejection! No stress! No embarrassment!

We love giving prospects the gift of another option for their lives.

Here is an example of the difference.

Imagine we own a restaurant. We stand outside our restaurant to solicit customers for our fine Italian cuisine. We stop a passerby and say, "We have the tastiest Italian food. Our chef comes from Sicily. She spent ten hours making her special tomato sauce. Do you want to come inside and eat?" Now this is a "yes" or "no," win or lose, live-or-die choice. We will feel bad if the passerby rejects us. There is risk.

Instead, imagine we stop a passerby and say, "If you feel like you want fine Italian food this evening, we have it. Or, if you would rather eat cold leftovers at home, that is okay also." This is an option. The passerby feels good. No pressure. But if the passerby would like delicious Italian food, he would choose us. And if the passerby did not want delicious Italian food, and would rather eat cold leftovers at home, we are okay. We offered our option. We did our job. We served the passerby. We don't feel bad or rejected.

The "I am not selling anything" approach.

"Hi, Mr. Prospect. I would like to get an appointment with you and I only need 20 minutes of your time. I am not selling anything."

Prospects were not born yesterday. They can smell a salesperson a mile away. They think, "I smell a liar. Turn on the salesperson alarm. Be skeptical. Try to avoid this lying salesperson."

When we are new to the business, we might think this is a good approach. But after thinking it through, it feels sleazy. Why? Because we are not being genuine with our prospects.

Is there a way to fix this? Yes.

We will use the notification principle from our previous books. If you haven't read them, here is the short explanation of the notification principle.

If we opened a traditional business such as a restaurant on Main Street, would we at least want to let our friends know? Yes. They may not want to come to our restaurant, but they may know people that would. We don't ask them to come, but if they are looking for a place to eat out in the future, we don't want to keep our business secret. Plus, they could feel offended if they found out that we didn't tell them.

How would we notify our friends? If they ask us what is new in our lives, we can tell them about our restaurant. We could mail a simple postcard. Or put it on our social media. This is natural and not sleazy.

Think about this. If we open a shoe store, we realize our friends probably won't need shoes today. But we would let them know we opened the store in case they need shoes in the future. Do they have to come to our store? No. Maybe our styles do not match their tastes, but we leave that decision up to them.

Tony Miehle has a great script that he uses for his new insurance agents. When a new insurance agent joins, they see themselves calling their friends and saying, "Hey, want to buy some life insurance from me?" That sounds like an opening for a horror movie. His new agents are understandably scared to call for appointments.

How does Tony fix this? He tells his new agents to be upfront and honest. His agents should ask their contacts for an appointment, not to sell insurance, but to show those contacts what they are doing. Then, if their contacts meet people in the future who need life insurance, they can refer these people to the new agent.

That is a much easier way to approach people. Most people are happy to take a few minutes to understand what we do. Then, if they meet someone who needs our products or services, they can send them to us.

Ready to see Tony's script? Here it is.

"I want to take a few minutes to show you what I am doing. I am not stopping by to sell you anything. But I would like you to be a referral source in the future in case you meet someone who could use my service. And, if you see something that interests you, that is okay too, but that is not the reason I want to come over and visit."

That is upfront and straight to the point. We give a reason for our appointment and explain why we are not there to sell to them. This helps relieve our prospects' stress. By giving a reason, this sounds more genuine and doesn't set off their salesman alarms.

Could we modify this for our business? Let's try one for a nutrition business.

"On Monday, I started my new health business. I know you are super healthy, so I am not asking you to buy anything. But I would like to show you what I am doing in case you meet people who are not as healthy as you, and they need help. Hopefully, you could refer them to me if you like what I show you. Do you have 10 minutes sometime later in the week?"

Yes, we are asking for 10 minutes of their time. But this isn't as scary as trying to make a sales appointment. The good news is they may like what we are doing so much, they may volunteer to be a customer. Or even a team member.

Do we feel better about this approach? Here's another advantage. Everyone we talk to knows at least 200 people that we don't. They can point us to someone who desperately needs our products or services immediately.

How about trying one for a travel business?

"Last week I started my new discount travel business. I know you don't travel much and seldom take holidays, but I did want to show you what I do. That way when you meet someone who wants to take a holiday, you can refer them to me. I will be able to save them a lot of money, and they might even write you a thank-you note. Your friends will appreciate it. I can bring you up-to-date in just a few minutes. When is the least hectic time for you this weekend to watch a short, four-minute video?"

Do prospects fear calls from us? Yes. But of all the types of calls we could make, asking for referrals scares them the least. Here are the three types of calls from our prospects' points of view:

#1. They will ask me to join their business. (The biggest fear.)

#2. They will ask me to buy something. (The second biggest fear.)

#3. They will ask me for referrals. (The smallest of the big fears.)

Here is some good news. Many people will be happy to help us in our new business. They will use their word-of-mouth conversations to promote us. Why? Because people feel good when they help someone. And the help they are giving us does not cost them anything. A real win-win for everyone.

Okay, feeling better now?

But what about our internal motivation?

Let's look at motivation next.

Motivation.

This is a rhetorical question.

Where do we get our best motivation?

A. Internally?

B. Externally?

Of course we all know the answer. Self-motivation, the kind that comes from inside us, is consistent every day.

How do we get this internal motivation?

Easy. Remember the previous case study of the three groups of salespeople? Remember how we used product and service customer stories to strengthen their beliefs and change their internal stories? These same stories can power our internal motivation.

Here is exactly what we should do to build our internal motivation. It is simple, but many skip this step and struggle.

If we sell life insurance, we should visit widows and families that lost their main source of income when the family's "bread earner" died. Listen to their stories of how much difference it made in their lives to have life insurance at that moment.

If we sell diet products, we can visit happy, thinner customers who improved their self-images and health by using our products. They could show us their new wardrobes. Or how they can now take long walks with their children.

What if we sell skincare that eliminates teenage acne? Wouldn't it be fun to hear the testimonials of teenage girls who dreaded going to school, but now feel confident with their flawless complexion?

What if we had doubts about our business opportunity? What can we do then? We would visit with successful distributors who changed their lives with new, well-paying careers in network marketing.

If we sell discount travel, wouldn't it be fun to visit with a family that just returned from Disney World? We could listen to their story of how they could never afford this before, but our company made it possible.

Each person we talk to creates a bigger belief. We build a better story and conviction inside of us. When that story and conviction is stronger, our discomfort about sharing our message goes away.

That is our goal. Remove the discomfort of sharing our message. And as a side benefit, we feel motivated after hearing how others' lives have improved.

Can our internal story destroy our motivation to talk to people?

Yes. Here is an example.

A company removed a certain bonus from its compensation plan. How did some people react?

"Oh no! This is terrible. They removed one of our bonuses. This is not as good as before. No one will join."

This is a typical emotional response to a very real event. The compensation plan is not as good as it was before.

But how good was the remaining compensation plan? Much better than when the company started. When the company started, the compensation plan was very basic. Yet, people saw opportunity and joined. And joined. And joined. Each year the plan added a little something extra. And people joined.

This year? The company removed one of the little extras. The compensation plan is still great, but some distributors told themselves a new story: "No one will join with the current plan."

Yes, the distributors made up this internal story: "No one will join without that extra bonus."

Could they create a new story in their minds? Yes. Let's help them tell themselves a new internal story now.

> "When our company started, we didn't even have brochures. Our compensation plan had only one way of getting paid. Over the years, we added 11 new ways of earning more bonuses. But even when we only had one way of getting paid, people joined our opportunity. They saw that joining our company could change their lives. They wanted that opportunity. Yesterday, our company removed one of those 11 new ways of earning bonuses. Now, there are only ten new ways to earn bonuses. This is so much better than when we started. Plus, now our company has stability and a good reputation. For new people joining today, this will be the most exciting opportunity of their lives."

Remember, it is all a story. A made-up story that we place into our minds.

We should now be thinking, "Stories are great! Can I use the same story technique to make it easier for prospects to join?"

Of course. Let's take a moment to see how that works.

If we are hesitant to call for an appointment, why? Do we have reservations inside our minds that our prospects might not benefit from our offer? In that case, let's fix it with a story. In our minds, we will create a "worst that can happen" scenario. And if our "worst that can happen" scenario is an improvement for our prospects' lives, we will feel confident about talking to them.

Two quick examples. One is for diet products. One is for utilities.

Here is how the new story for diet products would sound:

"When you join, and receive your box of our diet products, let me show you the worst that can happen. No one you talk to, not even your mother, wants to buy our diet products. Then you get busy at work and don't want to continue the business. Instead, you use your box of products and end up ten pounds lighter with more energy. Plus, you saved money by buying at the wholesale price. Can you live with the worst-case scenario?"

Wow. Most prospects would say yes to this, and they didn't even know any of the compensation plan benefits.

Okay, now let's look at the utilities story that we could tell our prospects.

"When you join, the worst that can happen is that you eventually get 50 people who want to save on their electricity. You can do this in 50 days, 50 weeks, 50 months. Your choice. Take as long as you want. But you will eventually find 50 people who want to pay less on their bill instead of paying more. Not everyone is bad at math, and they can figure out that paying less is better. Then you would have a $500-a-month pension. How good is that? And you didn't have to work and wait 40 years to get it. That is the worst that can happen when you join our business."

If we wanted, we could continue our stories with a little more positive hope. Here is an example.

"Now, if you decide to build a team, things get a whole lot better. Lots of instant bonuses and long-term bonuses. Most people who join decide they want to help their friends with a second paycheck. Their friends need it. And now they are helping their friends, and they get extra bonuses every month. You can build as big a team as you want. That is up to you."

We can solve most of our fear and internal motivation problems with this simple internal story technique. It may take a bit for our subconscious mind to accept the story, but it will with repetition. We can get our subconscious minds to believe almost anything with repetition. Now we can start taking control of our minds.

Appointments: "What we do FOR someone, not TO someone."

This is a good saying for us to remember. It puts our mindset in the right place. When we are doing something for other people, we naturally feel good. What are we doing that feels so good? Giving them one more option to improve their lives.

Our problem is that we get so excited about the benefits to us, we approach people with the intent of doing something TO them. We want to get them to buy from us, to join our business, to help us qualify for the next rank. Our enthusiasm takes over.

35

HOW TO GET APPOINTMENTS WITHOUT REJECTION

Prospects smell this. Then our actions appear ugly to them. We get rejected. We take it personally and feel bad.

Handling our fear and anxiety is an inside job. We should direct our thoughts and intentions to giving our prospects one more option to improve their lives.

Can I fake my intentions?

No. We must truly believe we are offering an option. Prospects know when we attempt to fake our intentions. How do they do this? They have sophisticated subconscious mind programs that quickly scan us for clues. Everyone has these programs. Even our pets can detect when we are not sincere!

So faking our intentions won't work. We must change our mindset from "It is all about me and what I can get," to "It is all about offering a wonderful option that prospects can choose to change their lives."

Communication is more than just words.

Stop "attempting" appointments with strangers.

Take a few moments to think about this statement.

Think about the "big picture" when attempting to get appointments with strangers.

Getting appointments with strangers is about what happens **before** we ask for the appointment.

No magic sentence or script? Nope.

Our success depends on what happens **before** we ask our prospects to set aside some time for us. Don't rely on a magic script to automate getting appointments.

So what are some of the other skill factors besides the words? We will learn them soon.

Let's move on now to what we say and do when we reach out to others.

Skills.

Our favorite part!

If our mindset is right, and we still don't get results, we have to face the obvious. Our lack of skills is holding us back. We have to improve our skills.

Saying dumb words such as, "I joined a new business opportunity, and would like to give you a sales presentation" is embarrassing. I know. You would never say something dumb like that. Keith and I wouldn't either. Okay, Keith wouldn't. I may have tried a few hundred times before I saw the trend. I'm a slow learner. :)

But if our skills are terrible, our positive attitude won't be enough to save us. Every little skill we learn makes us better.

The best way to learn skills?

First, here is the worst way.

Take a four-year course on cooking. Then, upon graduation, see a stove and an oven for the first time. Try to remember everything from our notes that we memorized. That is a formula for fear and terrible cuisine.

The best way to learn?

Yes, read books, take courses, and attend workshops. Short-cut the learning curve by leveraging other people's experiences. But, as we learn each new secret, go out and practice. That way the new secret becomes automatic.

We know it. We lived it. We don't have to remember. It is like driving a car or riding a bicycle.

Learn, practice, learn, experience, learn, try out, etc.

The big lesson.

Learning the skill and having good notes is only halfway to competency. Experience is necessary. We need to see how each part of a skill works in real life. We don't want to go out to talk to people and think, "I have a hunch this might work." No, we want real world experience, not hunches.

Here is another example for this important step. Our conscious mind can hold one thought at a time. If we read a book, attend courses, and watch car-driving videos, that is a lot to remember. Our conscious mind can't do it. We would sit in the car for the very first time, and then try to remember all the notes we took from a book. I am sure it would be an ugly experience.

When we learn something and then immediately practice, we get experience. We form some muscle memory. This means that our subconscious mind can remember this task automatically. We don't have to think about how to do it again. This is why we are so good at driving our cars today. Everything is automatic. We don't have to think of how hard to push the brake, or how to avoid over-steering in a corner.

We attempt some phrases. Experience how our prospects react. Consider how we respond. And next time, our answers will come quicker. Then, we can move on to more phrases.

Soon, we experience almost every possible response from prospects. No more surprises. No more wondering what to say.

When our experience reaches this level, we can take the next step up. What is that?

We concentrate our brain power on helping our prospects. We listen harder to what they say. This makes the difference between amateurs and professionals.

As we learn these appointment-getting skills, let's get real-life experience along our learning journey. It is too easy to sit at home and say to ourselves, "I have a feeling this sentence might work. I think my prospects might respond this way."

Real life. Real encounters. Now we will know what works for us, and what doesn't.

Don't skip this step!

The appointment skill secret our sponsors don't tell us.

The secret is "empathy." If we have empathy, calling prospects is fun and easy.

What is empathy? It is putting ourselves into our prospects' shoes. We try to think like they are thinking now. We attempt to understand things from their points of view.

With empathy, we can anticipate the possible objections. We listen for resistance, and pay close attention to the needs of our prospects. We learn their objections and can address those objections, before prospects have a chance to bring them up. Taking care of possible objections before they happen is good business. Taking care of objections after they happen requires salesmanship.

Empathy.

The first step of connecting is to know our prospects. That means to know our prospects' problems, their lives, their struggles and dreams. Need proof?

If we are accountants, we find it easy to talk to other accountants. Instant connection. We know what they are thinking. We feel their pain and frustrations. We know them even though we may have just met. We understand and have empathy.

This means our first step in connecting is to know our prospects. They will feel like we understand them. Now we are on our way to connecting for an appointment.

High-level appointment skills start with this understanding because it leads to an easy connection.

If we are an engineer, we find it comfortable to connect with other engineers. We understand them.

Should engineers attempt to call and connect to quilters, new-age fortune tellers, and the local candle club? Probably not. If we are already involved in one profession or interest, why not concentrate our time and efforts there?

The second step is to list the pains and frustrations of the people we have something in common with. How can we customize what we have to offer unless we know how we can reduce their pain and frustration?

An example?

Accountants. What are some possible pains and frustrations for accountants? Not every accountant will have all of these, but the more we know, the more presenting options we will have.

- Constant recertification every two years.
- Long hours for three months during tax submission season.
- Clients that have sloppy records.
- Poor advancement opportunities.
- Boring surroundings.
- Unrealistic expectation from clients.
- Too many details to keep track of.
- Tough commuting challenges to the city center.
- Repetition, repetition, repetition.

Okay, these are only a few to get us started. Now we understand their pains and frustrations. Will our accountant prospects be able to tell if we understand them and have empathy for their situation? Yes.

The third step? The words. The proper words will now flow to us effortlessly. We will know what to say for our ice breakers, our closes, and we can relate to any objections. We know their problems. We know how to offer our products and opportunity. We will connect with people instead of using a generic sales presentation for everyone. No one wants to be treated like a number. We want a connection.

Many networkers spend years attending hundreds of meetings and rallies, and yet no one tells them how to get appointments.

Getting appointments requires skill. Once we are past our close friends and relatives, it gets harder. We start from a position of no trust. Then we ask them to give us their valuable time.

And the fact that we want to sell them something makes it even harder. They notice.

With our mindset in place, when we are confident we provide value, it should be easy to get others to set an appointment, right?

No.

Let's look at what goes on in our minds every second of every day.

"Who fed the dog? I'd better plan dinner tonight. What will I wear tomorrow for work? How will I solve the big problem with our group project? Which show do I want to watch first tonight when I get home? Can we afford a family holiday now? Where can we go that isn't expensive? What if my spouse gets laid off? What if ..."

So many decisions, so little time. We can only handle one decision at a time. Other decisions pressure us to finish with our current decisions and to take them next. Yikes. Stress. We don't have time. And now some salesperson wants us to put all those important decisions on hold? We can't do that. These decisions are too important and we must act now.

Imagine these thoughts are in our mind. Now, the phone rings. Let's see how we interpret the caller's words. Ready?

Caller: "Hi. My name is Mr. Caller."

Us: (Stop my decision-making. Put all those decisions on hold for a second. What does this interrupting person want?)

Caller: "I just joined an exciting business opportunity ..."

Us: (Uh-oh. Salesman. Will try to sell me something. Be skeptical. Don't believe anything. Avoid his evil salesman manipulation.)

Caller: "And I only need 20 minutes of your time."

Us: (Huh? 20 minutes? Are you crazy! I can't put all these decisions on hold for 20 minutes! I can't even give you 20 seconds!)

Caller: "I want to give you a presentation."

Us: (Presentation?!!!!! That means a salesman for sure. Bolster the defenses. Hide. Run! Run! Save ourselves!)

Caller: "So when would be a good time for us to meet? Thursday at 3pm, or Friday at 6pm?"

Us: (Never.) "I am sorry. I am so busy. I don't have any time. We are moving. Yeah, leaving the country. I can't schedule another thing."

Empathy to the rescue!

Now imagine we're the caller. As professionals, we sense the interruption and stress in our prospect's voice. So, we immediately use one of our prepared responses to let our prospect know we understand.

Part of our experience will be observing the objections we encounter or create, and then have phrases to pre-empt the objections. This keeps the conversation friendly and pleasant. For example, for the "I don't have time now" objection, here are a few starters:

- "I interrupted what you are doing. I don't want to talk now. I just called to set a time when it is more convenient for us to talk."

- "Let's not talk now. You are busy. But, let's look at the best time for us to get together later."

- "Now might not be a good time to talk, and I need to let you get back to what you were doing. When is a more convenient time for you to talk for three minutes?"

- "I am sorry to catch you at a bad time. When is a good time to talk?"

- "Yikes. You sound super busy and I don't want to add to your stress. When is a good time for us to talk for three minutes?"

- "I know you are busy on a project right now. When is the least hectic time to call you back?"

- "I've only got a minute right now. I just wanted to know when would be a good time for a quick chat."

- "Sounds like you are tied up. I have some good news. When is a better time to call you?"

- "This might not be a good time to talk. When is the least hectic time to talk? When will you have about 3 minutes?"

Having these little phrases ready will not only reduce our personal fear, but also relax our prospects.

A little preparation with phrases can go a long way towards making our appointment-getting process pleasant.

The first seconds.

We call prospects for an appointment. How quickly will they decide if they want an appointment with us? Unfortunately, in the first few seconds.

So how soon should we put our problem-solving benefit into our conversation?

As soon as possible. With good friends we must be a bit social first, but with strangers, they want to hear our reason for calling first.

As we put our calling notes together, we want to have a huge list of possibilities. Then, when we do our research before calling, we have relevant problems and benefits we can address. Here are some possibilities.

Problems:

- Hard to get by on one paycheck.
- No time for the children.
- No chance for promotion.
- Terrible traffic commuting to work.
- Can't afford a decent holiday.
- Growing old.
- No energy.
- Acne.
- Perfumes are too expensive.

- Wrinkles.
- Children won't eat healthy.
- Worry about speeding tickets.
- Phone bills too high.
- Electricity prices in summer.
- Fat accumulates while sleeping.

Benefits:

- Get another paycheck.
- Control our time every day.
- Earn and advance on our efforts.
- Work from home.
- Discount luxury holidays.
- Keep our bodies young.
- More energy than a 3-year-old.
- Skin smoother than a baby's behind.
- Quality fragrances without the brand-name prices.
- Reduce wrinkles while we sleep.
- Concentrated salad in a capsule.
- A lawyer in your hip pocket.
- Lower phone bills.
- Lower electricity bills.
- Burn fat while we sleep.

We will need these in a future chapter as we start constructing exactly what we want to say. Eventually we will want others to send prospects to us. They will need to know why their friends and contacts should contact us. And thinking of these problems and benefits for the prospects puts us into a great state of mind.

The basic elements of
a phone script.

What will we say? We can't make calls based upon our attitude alone. We will eventually have to say something. We want to make sure our words do not trigger salesman alarms. Plus, we should assure our prospects that this initial call for an appointment will be short.

So first, let's use a little common sense before we rush into our first call.

To friends, don't start by saying, "How are you today?" This creates an unpleasant salesman odor that our friends smell. Or how about starting like this with someone we don't know?

"Hi, my name is John Doe and I am calling to see if ..." Does that sound like a sales call to you?

Want to cripple our start? Then sound like a cheesy salesman. We have pictures in our minds of plaid suit salesmen from the 1970s, going door-to-door, high-pressuring residents. Let's not go there. Here are some dated salesmen sayings we can avoid. We want to sound like real human beings instead of self-absorbed, selfish salespeople.

- "What is it going to take to put you into this business opportunity today?"
- "Is Tuesday at 3pm, or Wednesday at 5pm better?"
- "Well, aren't you interested in your family's future?" Yes, this borders on outright rude.

- "I am going to be in your neighborhood tomorrow, and I would like to pop by." What is our prospect thinking? "Pop by??? That sounds like a salesman. Plus, I don't sound very important."

So much for the bad scripts. Let's see what we can do.

Here is a script from phone professional Bernie De Souza. Feel free to adjust this to your personality and style. The script is very short, but very effective. Remember? Prospects want us to be short and to the point.

Bernie's script has five steps.

1. The opening words.

2. Mind-reading.

3. Create rapport with the prospect.

4. An ice breaker to create interest.

5. The close. Booking the meeting.

Bernie likes to use the word "meeting" instead of appointment. He says, "Appointments sound scary. Think of dentist appointments. Instead, the word 'meeting' seems softer." This is up to you and your potential prospects. However, being careful with words makes a huge difference.

Let's go through the steps one by one. We will pretend we are calling someone we already know.

#1. The opening words. "This is Bernie. Is this a good time for you?" Ten words. The prospects now know who is calling. Bernie makes sure now is a good time for the prospects to talk. Remember, if we are polite, other people will be polite.

#2. Mind-reading. "You are probably wondering why I am calling." Eight words. This shows that we are respectful and have empathy. And because Bernie read his prospects' minds, this helps build rapport. The prospects feel relieved. We announced that we are getting to the point immediately.

#3. Create rapport with the prospect. "Well, you know how ..." Four words. After the "Well, you know how" opening, we will tell our prospects about a problem they may have. These four words help foster agreement and rapport in someone's mind. Here are a few quick examples of how this would sound:

- "Well, you know how we both struggle with our weight?"
- "Well, you know how commuting to work is getting worse as traffic keeps piling up?"
- "Well, you know how we both want to take our families on holiday next year?"
- "Well, you know how we both hate our jobs?"

Prospects normally nod their heads in agreement, even though we may not see this on the call.

Could we use other words for instant rapport? Certainly. We could say, "I know you are busy." Acknowledging this fact makes our prospect feel better. We let our prospect know that we will not waste any time. We could do even better with some mind-reading, such as, "You are probably in the middle of a project."

#4. An ice breaker to create interest. "I just found out ..." plus our possible solution. Four words. How does that sound? Some examples:

- "I just found out how we can lose weight by changing our breakfast."
- "I just found out how we can work out of our homes instead of commuting."

- "I just found out how we can save money and pay whole-sale prices for our holidays."
- "I just found out how we can be our own boss."

This lets our prospects know why we want to talk to them. If we don't know the reason, we should do more research before we make the call. The reality is that our prospects will now make an instant decision if they are interested or not.

We can also create immediate interest with this. **"Are you …?"**

In our conversations with prospects, we can narrow their focus with this question, "Are you …?"

This keeps our conversations shorter, and more helpful too. Here are some examples:

- "Are you trying to save money on your electricity bill?"
- "Are you feeling tired in the afternoons?"
- "Are you tired of commuting early in the morning?"
- "Are you needing an extra paycheck every week?"
- "Are you wanting less expensive holidays for the family?"
- "Are you converting your home to more natural products?"
- "Are you interested in working from home instead of commuting?"

Talking in circles wastes time for both of us. Prospects appreciate it when we can get to the point immediately.

#5. The close. Booking the meeting. "Would it be okay if …" Five words. We will ask for the meeting (appointment). Here are some examples:

- "Would it be okay if we met Saturday morning?"
- "Would it be okay if we went to a meeting together?"

- "Would it be okay if we chatted via video Friday evening?"
- "You are busy all day. So, would it be best if we talked during lunch this week? So as not to interfere with your current busy schedule?"
- "We should talk. I respect that you have a full-time job, so is after work or weekends better for you?"

And ... that is it!

For someone we know, this is a great outline. For someone we don't know, of course, we will make a few adjustments. But, let's remember the important points.

- Be short.
- Get to the point.
- Be respectful.
- When we are polite, other people will be polite.

And then practice, practice, practice.

Why do we want to practice? Because without practice, prospects can smell uncertainty and desperation when we talk. That is why we must first have a good agenda, to help them. We want our prospects to feel that agenda, lower their defenses, and listen to our message.

A good exercise is to say these words immediately before calling. "I want to help this person. I will offer this person an option. Then, he or she can decide if this option fits in their life at this moment."

This way, if we make a mistake or forget what to say, the big impression we will leave is that we want to help them.

Is this the only formula for making calls to people we know?

No. There are many ways of calling for an appointment. The five-step formula is only one way. But the five-step formula helps us understand what our prospects would like to know next.

If you have read our other books, you know that the following script is one other way of calling for an appointment:

"I am perfectly comfortable with your decision to look at my business or not. But I was uncomfortable not asking if you wanted to look, and having you think that I didn't care."

This comfortable/uncomfortable approach makes everyone feel great. First, let's talk about us. We are not asking them to join or buy. We said that if we kept our business a secret, we wouldn't feel good. This creates a reason for our call. Now the call makes sense to the prospect. Because we are offering the option to listen to us or not, there is no chance of rejection for us.

Second, let's look at the prospects' points of view. How do they feel? Flattered, of course. They feel honored that we wanted to talk to them and not keep it a secret. In a way, they feel like they're part of our inner circle. Also, we gave our prospects a ready-made excuse to opt out of our conversation. They don't have to lie to get rid of us. They can say, "Thank you for caring. I don't have an interest right now, but I appreciate that you thought of me."

However, in most cases they will want to listen. Their curiosity is a powerful driving force. Can we imagine what a version of this would sound like if we called someone that we didn't know? Imagine we were calling a "lead" that we didn't know. We could open our conversation with the statement:

"You answered our ad and filled out a form for more information. I am perfectly comfortable if you changed your mind in the meantime. But I did want to call you right away because I didn't want you to think we didn't appreciate your request."

What a nice way to start a phone call with the stranger. It takes the pressure off both of us.

This comfortable/uncomfortable approach gets to the point immediately. Our prospects can make an immediate decision if they are interested or not. We won't waste our time, our prospects don't waste their time, and everyone is happy. No rejection, no hard feelings.

Should we keep going?

Yes! This is fun.

What if we create resistance, fear, or skepticism when we reach out for an appointment? Then we need some phrases to calm the situation. Here are two of our favorite phrases for doing this.

Imagine our prospects are resistant. We can immediately say:

"Relax. You don't have to take action on anything from this phone call. Let me give you the short story now, and that will leave you with some options for your future." This usually dissolves the stress and fear.

Here are more ways of diffusing the tension:

- "Does it make sense to cover everything here in the next 60 seconds? Then you can make an instant decision if this will benefit you?" The promise of only 60 seconds makes our prospect smile.

- "Let's quickly find out if this is a fit for you."
- "I know you are busy, so I will be brief."
- "Would a short email conversation make more sense?" (Use this if we detect major resistance.)

Persistence. When our dream isn't their dream.

Can't we just get motivated and not bother with scripts and empathy? Instead, why can't we rely on persistence and personal drive?

Here is why. Even if we are so motivated that we levitate up to someone, we will still have to say something. Prospects take note of our words when deciding to give us an appointment or not.

Our agenda is not to run their lives for them, but to add one more option. For some, their plans are set. For others, they welcome better options. We want to be there for the prospects looking for better options.

Not everyone will want to join our business, or even set an appointment, no matter how motivated and persistent we are. The world doesn't revolve around us and our needs.

However, let's look at what we offer. Is it a good value? Can it change prospects' lives? Will it help others? Of course. And that is why we offer it to others. We don't need to be disappointed when they don't take our offer. It isn't their time. And maybe their time will never come.

But with almost 8 billion people on our planet, there will be plenty of people in our market who we can serve.

What if I don't know anything about my prospect?

That is a difficult appointment call to make. Why would we call a prospect without doing our research first?

Possibly our research turned up nothing. Making cold calls like this can still work, but the secret is to get prospects to talk about themselves as soon as possible. When prospects are busy talking, telling their pent-up stories, we build a bit of rapport. But more importantly, we listen for suggestions of potential problems that we can solve.

So ask these prospects an engaging question. They love to talk about themselves.

When we isolate a clear problem we can help with, we can say, "I can help with that problem. I am sure you are busy now. Let's set a time when we can talk about that. Does next week work for you?"

Need some questions? Here are a few that will get a response.

- "Ever think about working full-time from home?"
- "Are you interested in working for yourself, or would you rather have a boss?"
- "Would you like a chance to get paid on your performance instead of being paid by the hour?"
- "What are you doing already to stay healthy?"
- "Do you find growing old really hurts?"

- "Would you like the chance to get tax deductions like companies do?"

But we are only getting started. Use your imagination for your business. Prospects love to talk about themselves. It is easy to get them started.

Making calls for appointments.

Voicemail after voicemail. Finally someone answers, and how do they respond to our call? They shut us down immediately with statements such as:

> "I am at work. Call me at another time."

> "Email me your information. Or email me your website."

> "Are you a salesman?" Click.

> "Take me off your list!"

> "Who told you to call me?!!!"

> "I don't care what you are selling, I am not interested."

Expectations.

Our first job is to manage our expectations. Our call will be an interruption in someone's day. That is the nature of a call. We won't feel bad about interrupting someone's day if our call is short.

Now, what can we expect? When our prospects receive the call, what is the current state of their lives?

- Will they be busy with their children?
- Will they be worrying about their current problems?
- Are they bored from watching television?
- Were they daydreaming?
- Were they busy making meals for the week?

- Is this the perfect day for them to join our business?
- Is this the perfect minute for them to talk to us extensively?
- Were they thinking about that very problem we can solve?

Chances are, no. The odds of us calling someone at the perfect moment, on the perfect day, when they were considering their problems and looking for solutions, are pretty slim. That would be a very lucky call.

Now, we understand the law of averages. Not everyone on every day will smile and take our call. Some people are having bad days. Some people are too busy. We understand that if we make ten calls, only a few will answer, and from those few we will get an appointment or two. Realistic expectations keep us from discouragement. A little empathy for the busy days of others goes a long way.

The reality is that most people who want to solve their problems will welcome our call, and would be happy to set a good time to talk. We can fulfill their request by setting an appointment when it convenient for them. This is called being polite.

This means our call should be short. We get to the point, and our prospects will be happy. Remember, the purpose of the call is to set an appointment, not to give an entire presentation.

And most importantly, we should adjust our expectations. Not everyone we call can be in the state of mind to instantly join. Other people have lives, too.

Circumstances change.

Will we get discouraged? Yes. But if we manage our expectations, we will overcome our bad days.

One way to overcome discouragement is with the "moving parade" principle. Imagine we are standing on the side of the street and a parade is slowly marching by. This means a different group of people is in front of us every 30 seconds. This is like prospecting. New people become prospects every day.

Looking for new people to join our business opportunity? Every year millions of people turn 18. This is a brand-new group for us to market our business opportunity to. Every year we get a new group.

And what happens within a group? People have changes in their circumstances every day. Some get new jobs, some lose jobs. Some get married. Others look for career changes. We could talk to someone who isn't ready to buy or join today, but next month they might have a different view of the future.

So if some prospects say "no" today, that does not mean "no" forever. And if they have no interest right now? A new group of prospects is walking behind them in the parade. Prospects are everywhere.

Want a better chance to get appointments?

Most prospects have today planned. Tomorrow? Not so much. Next week? Hardly at all.

If we ask for an appointment today or tomorrow, our prospects will likely have to reschedule something important to them. The further into the future that we make the appointment, the less likely our prospects will have an important engagement scheduled.

Of course, the downside is that our prospects forget about the appointment if it is too far in the future.

But a good rule to remember is: "The further the appointment is into the future, the less resistance we will get."

What can I say when I leave a voicemail?

First, some quick examples of messages we can leave.

- "Well, looks like now doesn't seem to be a good time to talk. Let's try again Thursday at 6pm. Let me know if that doesn't work out well for your schedule."

- "I promised to call you back. I didn't want you to think I forgot and abandoned you. Obviously you are busy right now, so I will call back tomorrow at the same time."

- "Missed you. So I will send you a copy of what happened to Mr. Jones. He had the same problem you have, and he fixed it. I will call you tomorrow after you have a chance to read it."

- "Hey, remember me? I promised to call you when we met at the networking breakfast. Looking forward to our visit."

Okay, now we have a few messages we can say so that we don't get caught by surprise and say, "Uh, uh. Well. Uh, uh I see you are not home and I uh, uh, wanted … no wait, uh, uh …"

But we can do better than this.

Let's ask ourselves, "Why don't people call us back?"

And the answer is, "Because they don't want to talk to us!"

Not the answer we want to hear, but sometimes reality is harsh.

Nobody wants to call and listen to a sales presentation. Nobody volunteers to waste their time on something with unknown benefits.

We must give prospects a reason to call us back. The better the reason, the better chance we have of getting an appointment to talk with them in more detail.

As we know, our busy minds have hundreds or thousands of decisions waiting their turn. Something must show a quick and clear benefit for us to prioritize it now. So instead of being like ordinary long-winded salespeople, we will deliver. Want some ideas?

- "I am starting my own business and I want to do it with you."
- "I decided to live longer, and I wanted you to join me."
- "I decided to finally do something about my wrinkles, and thought you might want to also."
- "I enjoyed working at home the last three months. Now I want to make it permanent. What about you?"

Or, we can start the conversation with a benefit immediately. Here are some examples:

- "I am calling to see if I can help with your organization's fundraising." Every non-profit organization needs help.
- "I am calling to see if you would like to add some employee benefits for your workforce. These employee benefits won't cost you anything." It is easier to commit when it is free.
- "We are in the same aerobics class. Would you like to know how to keep our fat-burning exercise working longer, even days after our last session?"

- "I don't think we will keep our telephone booth manufacturing jobs much longer. Want to check out another career option with me?"

- "Your friend, John, said you were just like me, always looking for a way to get ahead. Would you like to know how I am doing that?"

- "I know you are busy now, but when can you spend 12 minutes to lower your electric and gas bill?"

- "You are already busy with a family and full-time job. When can we talk for 10 minutes so I can help you get some more free time?"

One or two sentences. To the point. And our prospects can make instant decisions from their voicemail messages. We have to get to the front of the decision-making queue in their minds.

The first thing we should do to make our short messages better is to make them ... shorter. Feel the difference in our minds between the longer and the shorter statements.

Long: "This book can show you have to overcome the fear of getting appointments, reset our mindset, how to focus on the problems of our prospects, with easy to learn phrases ..."

Short: "70 years of appointment-setting tips in one short book."

Long: "With the recent utility deregulation act, our company has secured long-term discount contracts with the major providers, and can pass significant savings on to you."

Short: "We can make your utilities bills lower in about 15 minutes."

Long: "Do you keep your income options open? This is a great way to diversify your income while building a long-term residual income, without risking your present job."

Short: "Can you use an extra paycheck as early as next Friday?"

Did we notice some missing phrases? We didn't use words and phrases such as:

- "Get together and chat." (Who has time to chat mindlessly with a salesperson?)

- "Just checking in with you." (This doesn't sound very important at all.")

- "I am going to be in your area next week and was wondering …" (Oh my. This doesn't sound urgent or important. Let me get back to my decisions.)

Do we see the difference? When we see things from our prospects' viewpoints, it is clear. We have to state a benefit immediately. Here are some more short examples of what we can say to get action from our prospects.

- "I know you still work nights, but would you like to change careers so you don't have to sleep during the day?"

- "I am just curious. Would you like an extra paycheck once a month to help with those school fees?"

- "I am fixing my fading memory. Can I tell you about what I am doing?"

- "I got tired of the grandkids making fun of my wrinkles. I want to tell you my plan."

- "I got my son's college tuition bill today, but this time I didn't worry. You and I should talk."

- "Do you still get monthly electricity bills? I want to tell you what I am doing."

- "I just got done lowering my gas bill. Thought of you. When can we talk?"

- "Do you want more employee benefits to make them happier? Especially if you don't have to pay for the benefits?"

- "I am just curious. Would you like to go back to working at home?"

- "Are you still dieting? You've got to try this. When can we talk?"

- "Still going to the local coffee shop every morning? Call me back. I have something even easier."

Seeing a trend?

All we have to do is think, "Bottom line, what is in it for my prospects?" Then, tell them right away. They will make a snap decision if this is good for them now, or not.

The purpose of the call is to get an appointment.

Us: "Hi. Would you hurry up and buy? I don't want to go through my entire sales presentation."

Okay, we would never do this, but we are selfish and impatient. Do we ever feel that we would like to complete the entire sale immediately? Every time!

Our prospects are not as familiar as we are with our companies. They need time. Let's avoid the big mistake of trying to close the sale on our initial call, instead of getting the appointment.

Professional realtors have a strategy. When they run an ad for a house for sale in the local newspaper, they are not trying to sell the house. Instead, they are trying to sell the reader on calling them. The focus is getting the phone call.

How do they do this?

They show a picture of the house. Below the house they give the details. But, they don't give all the details. They always leave out one big detail that people will have to call to get. For most buyers in the United States, there are three big factors when choosing a home.

- How much will this home cost?
- How many bedrooms does it have?
- Where is it located?

Those three questions filter the thousands of houses advertised.

Realtors will choose to put two of these three factors into the advertising. If the first two factors are interesting, the interested buyer will call to get the third factor. Now, the realtor has a prospect to talk to.

They don't make the mistake of attempting to sell the house in the newspaper. Not much chance of doing that anyway. They focus on an opportunity to talk more.

It is the same for us. The purpose of our call is to get the opportunity to talk more. Amateurs try to do all of their selling in the first phone call. Professionals set a time when they can talk leisurely, with less stress, and at a better communication level.

Can I get appointments by text or messaging?

Yes!

Many people hide behind their phones to avoid salespeople. Why do people do this? Because they only have 24 hours in a day. If they spent their entire day listening to salespeople, they wouldn't have time to eat.

Plus, they are afraid that salespeople will talk them into doing something they don't want to do. The best way to avoid this is to not talk to them. They limit their communication to texts, messaging, and emails. And if that doesn't keep salespeople away, they lie. They say things such as, "I didn't get your text. Your email went to my spam folder. I haven't had a chance to check my messages in days. My phone broke. Somebody hacked my account."

People have fear for good reason. The downside to this fear? They push away opportunities to improve their lives.

Our solution? To send a text or message that will compel them to talk to us.

Texting for appointments.

If we didn't notice earlier, short voicemail messages are also perfect to use when we text.

Why do we text prospects when we can call them directly?

For some prospects, texting is appropriate. That is how some prospects expect us to communicate with them.

Sending out the text is easy. Many will be ignored. No personal rejection. We take the hint. Other texts will get a reply, "Please tell me more." That's a good sign. We can text back, "Let's talk. When is a good time?" Done.

The problem with texting for appointments.

We text back and forth and hope they understand our messages. Sometimes they won't understand our text or intention. To avoid this, we want to get prospects on the phone or a video call. Why?

Because text messages are too easy to misinterpret. Texting is low-level communication. Prospects don't hear our tone of voice. They can't see our facial expressions. They won't read our body language. They can't even see if we are smiling!

Here is an example of prospects misinterpreting what we say.

Us: "This is so easy. You can do it."

How might our prospect interpret this?

- Do you think I am dumb?
- Don't you know I don't have time?
- Wait, if it is so easy, why do you need me?
- What do I need to do? Sounds like there is a catch.

A better strategy is to use texting to get an appointment to talk on the phone. At least talking on the phone will give us better communication, with less misinterpretation. Here is an example.

Us: "Can I call you right now? It will only take three minutes."

Do presentations take longer than three minutes? Sometimes. If it takes longer, it should be because they ask us to continue. Now it is their decision. They are asking questions and getting engaged in the presentation. No one wants a boring lecture.

Here are a few more examples of quick texts or messages.

Us: "Let's discuss this over a video call and coffee."

Prospects can be a block away, a mile away, or even in a different country. They can easily hop on a video call with us. Why coffee? Prospects feel comfortable when they have a drink in their hand or something that makes them feel social. We can choose whatever beverage works best for our demographic. Many of our relatives may prefer a beer.

Us: "Grab a cup of coffee. Let's see if this is a fit for you. I will call you in five minutes to give you a chance to grab your coffee."

"A fit for you" doesn't sound too intimidating. No pressure. And their curiosity might say, "Yes. I want to know how this works."

Us: "I know you are busy. It will only take seven minutes to see if this works for you or not. Then you will never have to think about it again."

Us: "Don't worry about setting aside a time. We can do this right away and be done in three minutes."

Us: "You are busy. I don't want to waste your time, so let's go over this in three minutes so you can decide."

What else could we say in a message?

Keith likes to use rhetorical questions. These questions usually bring a "yes" answer. To start his text, he will use, "I am just curious." This phrase softens the approach, and makes prospects feel more comfortable.

Next, he uses an instant decision-prompting close. He says, "Would it be okay if …?" These five words normally prompt a "yes" response in our prospects' minds.

Next, he inserts a great benefit that could help the prospect.

Let's put these three steps together and make some interesting messages.

- I am just curious. Would it be okay if you had an easy option to work four days a week, instead of five?

- I am just curious, would it be okay if you had an extra paycheck every month?

- I am just curious, do you drink coffee? Would it be okay if your coffee helped you lose weight?

- I am just curious, would it be okay if you could work out of your home instead of commuting?

- I am just curious, would it be okay if you could lose weight just by changing what you eat for breakfast?

- I am just curious, do you know how to protect your name and accounts from identity theft? Would it be okay if it was easy?

- I am just curious, would it be okay if you could make your skin smoother while you sleep?

- I am just curious, are you still dieting? Would it be okay if you tried something that would make it quicker?

- I am just curious, do you find that growing old really hurts? Would it be okay if there was a way to slow it down?

- I am just curious, would it be okay if you could get fitter without going to the gym?

- I am just curious, would it be okay if you had an option for a higher-paying career?

Now, we put our whole message in one text. But there is another way. We could talk more about the problem first, and then reply with, "Would it be okay if ...?" Watch this:

Us: "I am just curious, does your body hurt after your workouts?"

Prospect: "Yes."

Us: "Would it be okay if you had something to fix that?"

• • •

Us: "I am just curious, do you still hate your job?"

Prospect: "Yes."

Us: "Would it be okay if I showed you one more option tomorrow?"

• • •

Us: "I am just curious, would you like to top off your pension with an extra check?"

Prospect: "Of course."

Us: "Would it be okay if I show you what I am doing?"

• • •

Us: "I am just curious, do you ever get speeding or parking tickets?"

Prospect: "Yes, too many."

Us: "Would it be okay if I showed you an easy option to reduce them or get out of them entirely?"

• • •

Us: "I am just curious, do you still get electricity bills every month?"

Prospect: "Of course. They know where I live."

Us: "Would it be okay if those bills were lower?"

• • •

Us: "I am just curious, do you find it hard to get a raise at work?"

Prospect: "A raise? I am lucky to keep my job."

Us: "Would it be okay if I show you how to get paid more?"

• • •

Us: "I am just curious, do you ever feel tired in the afternoons?"

Prospect: "Tired? I still feel exhausted even after my afternoon nap!"

Us: "Would it be okay if you could fix that?"

This pattern is so natural and easy. The prospects can answer "yes" or "no" from the safety of their phones or computers. Plus, if they want to fix their problem, they tell us. Now we feel better about setting the appointment. We want to help them.

Let's do a few more to get our creative thinking going.

Us: "I am just curious, do you ever feel stress?"

Prospect: "Stress? I live with stress. My husband is a carrier."

Us: "Would it be okay if you could get rid of your stress, without getting rid of your husband?"

• • •

Us: "I am just curious, do your kids still plan to go to university?"

Prospect: "Yes. I am selling my blood every three weeks to save up for it."

Us: "Would it be okay if I showed you another way of paying for their university tuition?"

• • •

Us: "I am just curious, do you still plan to take the family to Disney World next year?"

Prospect: "Yes. The children got tired of us just showing them the brochures."

Us: "Would it be okay if I showed you how to get a discount on that trip?"

• • •

Us: "I am just curious, are there a lot of sick kids at your children's school?"

Prospect: "Yes. Our school district is a petri dish for every known virus and bacteria."

Us: "Would it be okay if I show you how to help the kids develop better immune systems?"

• • •

Us: "I am just curious, does your mother still have wrinkles?"

Prospect: "Yes. They are getting so deep they are creating shadows."

Us: "Would it be okay if I showed her how to make them smaller?"

• • •

Us: "I am just curious, do you find it hard to remember things as we get older?"

Prospect: "All the time."

Us: "Would it be okay if I showed you what we could take to make our brains healthier?"

• • •

Us: "I am just curious, are you interested in working for yourself, or would you rather have a boss?"

Prospect: "I'd much rather work for myself! My dream-sucking vampire boss is taking little bits of my brain out every day, turning me into a human zombie!"

Us: "Would it be okay if you and I talk later about another option?"

We should have this pattern in our brains by now.

What can we reply next? It could be as easy as saying, "Let's talk."

The hard part is done.

Remember, we are selling the appointment, not our product, service, or business. It should be short.

Turn our future appointments into instant appointments.

It happens to us all. Our prospect says, "Oh yeah! That would be awesome!" Then when the appointment time comes, that prospect goes missing. Something comes up. His schedule changes. He won't reschedule. He's not excited anymore.

If we sense the excitement is high, instead of setting a future appointment, let's try to talk now.

#1. Try for a conversation first. Then attempt the appointment in later messages.

#2. Messaging is low-level communication. It strips the messenger from the conversation. Work towards moving the communication to a higher level such as a phone call, a video call, or an in-person meeting.

#3. By understanding prospects, we can create curiosity, and then our prospects will reach out to us for more information.

#4. Work towards an appointment, not towards a sale. Keep our materials to ourselves at this point.

Before we start, think about dating. We want to use the same courtesy as we would if we were asking for a date. An example?

I got an email. This stranger hoped I would be a great prospect for his business. His cold email contained … everything! Every detail. This is like telling someone our life's story on the first date. At least an email is easier to read than a text message. Long messages don't work. Let's save the effort for something important.

Sending a link to join on the first message? Presumptuous, and of course, not effective.

What about sending a link to a video or website? Would we do that when looking for a date? I don't think so. Imagine a potential sponsor saying, "You are a number, just another lead to me. I thought about talking to you as a person, but I didn't feel you were worth it. Go invest your personal time in watching my company video. If you are interested, get back to me. Maybe then I will feel that you are worth communicating with."

Then what could I say to turn this encounter into an instant appointment?

- Let's grab a quick five-minute bite in the breakroom. (Office scenario.)

- I want to get your thoughts on my idea. Can I call you in one minute?

- Now is a good time for me to talk briefly. What about you?

- Let's save ourselves some time. Can I call you now?

- Is now the best time for us to talk?

- Let's talk now.

Many prospects find it less painful to talk now than to push that pain into the future. All we have to do is ask.

It is not the list!

You may have heard of CRM, or Customer Relationship Management.

A network marketing company introduces their brand-new Customer Relationship Management system for prospecting. Distributors can now enter their leads into this high-tech piece of software. After some training, the distributor can sort their leads, rank their leads, set up alarms to re-contact certain leads, arrange leads by location, and make individual notes about their leads.

But it gets better! They can send automatic messages, print out reports, and have a ready-to-go list every morning of who they should contact that day. The software does amazing things and with more training, it seems almost a miracle. The team spends endless hours in wonder at the magic of technology. And every hour spent using the software feels as though they are building their empire.

And then someone asks the distributor, "And when you call your prospect, what are you going to say?"

Dead silence.

Finally, the distributor mumbles, "Uh, uh, I guess I will sort of change what I say depending on what the prospect says?"

Ouch.

All this data entry, sorting, arranging, scheduling … none of this matters to the prospect. None of this matters to the results.

When we contact prospects, they don't care if we spent hours or days playing with our prospect-tracking computer programs. They care about what we say and do.

Take this test.

Write down exactly, word-for-word, the first sentence we will say when we talk to our prospects on the phone. (If we are looking for excuses not to do this already, this is a big problem.)

Most distributors can't do this.

But it gets worse.

Write down exactly, word-for-word, the second sentence we will say. Now, most distributors will want to change the subject and talk about something else. This is not comfortable. We have excuses such as, "It depends. Everyone is different. I change it a lot. I make it up and adjust as I go. Depends if I know them or not. Or if they uh, uh, uh ..."

And now ... how about sentence #3? Ouch!!!!

Try this out. Let's tell our team member, "On a piece of paper, right now, write down the first five sentences you will say to your prospect when you call."

Then wait. And wait. And wait.

Ignore the excuses. Let the team member write or sweat. Yes, this is uncomfortable. But if this is uncomfortable now without the pressure of the prospect waiting on the other end of the phone, think how much more pressure we will feel when our prospect is waiting for our words.

What results should we expect? At best, maybe one or two sentences? At that point, we know it is time to start learning exactly what to say and do.

Is there anything wrong with spending hours with software programs that help us organize leads that we don't know how to talk to? No!

But we are missing the big picture. Talking to prospects effectively has nothing to do with these programs. It is how we connect and communicate that counts. Network marketing is a relationship business. We should never forget that.

Should I just buy leads and then call them for appointments?

Mike Miller and I were having dinner, and our conversation turned to buying leads, funnels, and attraction marketing. Now, Mike uses these tools effectively because when he gets a lead, he knows exactly **what** to say.

He asked me my thoughts on distributors and leads. My answer?

I tell distributors to never buy leads until they can answer my questions.

These are questions I use to check if they are ready to talk to cold prospects. If they don't know the answers, they aren't ready. They will only ruin the leads. I ask:

- "What are your first three sentences, word-for-word?"
- "If your prospect is skeptical, do you have at least five micro-phrases you will use to build instant rapport?
- "If your prospect doesn't believe you, which phrase will you use next?"
- "Which phrases will you use to command your prospects' brains to listen to you?"

- "What is your word-for-word close?"
- "What is your best one-sentence close?"
- "If your prospect wants to think it over, what is your next sentence?"
- "If your prospect asks for more information, what are your next two sentences?"
- "If your prospect asks to go to a website, what exactly will you say next?"
- "When your prospect wants to talk about his personal drama, what will you say next?"

Now, if the new distributor can't even answer these basic questions, why would this new distributor even want to be talking to cold prospects or leads?

The new distributor should not be looking for new prospects to ruin.

The new distributor should be learning what to say first.

Think about how much confidence we would have if we could clearly answer the above questions. When we feel confident, prospects notice.

"I still can't bring myself to ask others for an appointment."

If we are too shy to reach out for an appointment, we shouldn't give up on our careers. Why not let other people call us? Here is an example of learning and applying the skill of getting others to call us.

A young lady loved her dog. A lot. There are millions of dog lovers just like her. However, there is one thing about her dog she didn't like: picking up the poop in her backyard. Dog owners know that after a few weeks, the dog poop accumulates and someone has to pick it up. Dogs don't volunteer for this task.

The young lady thought, "I wonder if other dog lovers have these same mixed feelings about their dogs and the accumulated dog poop?" From this idea, a business was born.

The young lady decided to start a local "dog poop pickup business."

Some challenges:

First, not everyone would hire her. They could save money by picking up their own dog's poop in their backyard.

Second, where could she find some dog owners that would willingly pay someone to do this smelly job?

Third, that is a lot of dog poop to pick up. She would have to pay someone to do all the dirty work. That would cost more money. She would have to get a lot of clients.

Fourth, how could she get the word out about her new service and reach dog owners that would be great prospects for her?

Let's talk about the **first problem.** Yes, many people want to save money and pick up their own dog's poop. That group is not her market. Trying to get appointments, hard-core sales presentations, follow-up, and educating this group is far too time-consuming and expensive.

Second problem? Easy to solve. Find dog owners with money. She has to get her service in front of the owners who take their dogs to the veterinarian. Veterinarians charge a lot of money. These dog owners could afford her service.

Third problem? If she had a lot of customers, she could hire or subcontract the dog poop pickup to someone else. That's right. She could watch television while someone else did the actual pickup work. This problem solves itself with enough customers.

Fourth problem? How could she get in front of the veterinarian's customers? Well, it would be tacky to stand in front of the veterinarian's office. Plus that would be time-consuming. Instead, she could leave her business cards and flyers at each veterinarian's office. Her service does not interfere with the veterinarian's business in any way. Plus, it is a nice complementary service that many customers would like.

But, how to get an appointment with the veterinarian? No need to. All she needed to do was talk to the receptionist or veterinarian's assistant. Leave a box of her business cards and a stack of flyers. And to encourage more personal recommendations from the assistant, bringing a box of donuts with the business cards and flyers would certainly help.

Now, this young lady can sit back and wait for her phone to ring with pre-sold customers. It would be easy to get appointments.

The lesson?

If we have something of value, or if we solve a nasty problem, people will come to us for a solution. No resistance. No skepticism. Just pre-sold customers reaching out to us.

If people don't come to us fast enough, we can turbocharge the flow. How?

Remember the dog poop lady? She gave donuts and flyers to the receptionist. But she could do more. She could invite the receptionist to lunch. They could chat about how much some pet owners would appreciate a poop pickup service. Maybe the owners would thank the receptionist for her concern and service. Now the receptionist can provide extra service for the clinic's visitors.

Here are some referral examples to help us think of what we can do for our business.

- The coupon-collecting expert can refer friends to a financial advisor.
- The aerobics instructor can refer students to the food supplement distributor.
- The HVAC (heating, ventilation, and air conditioning) installers can refer customers to the discount utilities distributor.
- The expensive dress shop can refer customers to the high-end skincare distributor.
- The school principal can refer parents to the discount holiday distributor.

- The natural sandal sales clerk can refer customers to the natural cleaning products distributor.
- Tax preparers can refer clients who want a part-time business for income and tax-deduction opportunities.
- Car salesmen can refer people who need more income to qualify for the car of their dreams.

So let's ask ourselves this question:

"What is the huge problem that we solve?"

If the problem is big enough, our best prospects will come to us. Here are some examples of problems that people might have.

- High utility bills.
- Can't afford to take the family to Disney World.
- Tired of feeling tired.
- Hate looking at their wrinkles.
- Disgusted with their current lives.
- Long commutes to work.
- Want more opportunity in their lives.
- Find dying early inconvenient.

They want to fix these problems. They look for solutions, and that means us.

Is there an easier way to get incoming, pre-qualified customers?

What if making calls to get appointments feels completely out of our comfort zone? If that is the case, would it be better if others called us? Yes. Let's continue our ideas from the last chapter.

Would we like to have prospects reaching out to us every week, or even every day, wanting to talk to us? Of course this won't happen overnight, but we can create a steady flow of prospects reaching out to us.

The first thing we will need is a book, audio, video, or some sort of educational tool to give to prospects. What could this tool look like?

This tool is not to explain or sell our business. Instead, we want our tool to compel the user to reach out and contact us. Perhaps our tool educates them about a certain benefit of our products. If our service saves them money, the tool could motivate them to expand their financial goals. If our tool talks about changing careers, now we have prospects for our business opportunity.

The good news is with enough tools out there, we can have a steady stream of people contacting us.

One good thing about a generic tool is that it won't trigger salesman alarms in cold prospects. If it is a company tool, or branded to our product or service, then it will be perceived as a brochure or advertising. This raises skepticism. No one gets excited about receiving sales literature. However, prospects will appreciate it if we give them a generic educational tool that can enhance our lives.

Let's use a few book examples.

Keith wrote a book called *Why You Need to Start Network Marketing: How to Remove Risk and Have a Better Life*. This does a more direct job of helping prospects get involved in network marketing.

Want something a bit less direct? *Rich Dad Poor Dad*, by Robert Kiyosaki.

Or how about something that is so generic that no one could ever take offense?

The Richest Man In Babylon by George Clason teaches money management to first-timers in a relaxing story. Let's use this book for our example. It is inexpensive and a short read for our prospects.

We start by purchasing five paperback copies of the book. We will loan these out, one at a time, pick them up, and continue rotating these five books to new readers. What can we expect?

Some potential prospects will lose the book. Many won't read the book. Others will return the book with no comment. But from a few, we will receive a voicemail message that sounds like this:

"Thank you for loaning me this book. I finished reading it. Now I see why you like it. Can we meet again sometime next week for coffee or lunch? I would like to know a little more about what you do."

Will prospects overwhelm us with these calls? No. But the more books we loan out to quality prospects, the more calls we can expect.

If we are shy, we might think, "How will I loan out this paperback book?" Could we save money and send prospects to an electronic version of the book, a video on YouTube, etc.? Yes, but that leaves an impression of lower value with our prospects. If there is no effort on our part, our gift loses the appearance of value.

But let's continue with this paperback book example. We can apply the same principles to whatever we decide to use as a tool.

Giving this book to prospects allows us to put their interests first. We feel better, and of course, our prospects feel better also. Whether our prospects decide to join our network marketing business or not, by giving them this book, we know that we gave them a chance to change their lives. It is easier to give this book when we focus on our prospects' needs.

What if our prospects have no interest in network marketing or improving their money management? Who knows? They might find something else in the book helpful. The act of loaning prospects the book builds our "know, like, and trust" factor with them. It could turn an ice-cold prospect into a warm prospect, easier to talk to.

Here are a few opening statements we can use to interest our prospects before offering them a copy of this book:

- "I have been reading up on how to take control of my finances ..."

- "I just read this book and learned how to ..."
- "I have this book you can borrow. I wish I'd read this book in high school."
- "There might be something of interest for you in this book ..."
- "This book made a huge difference in my life ..."

To relieve any tension, we could say:

- "This book may or may not work for you."
- "This may or may not be what you are looking for, but it helped me a lot."

Reading a book is a commitment. There is no need for us to push people to take the book. If we force a book on them, they won't read it. Instead, leave it as an option for prospects who want to change their lives.

Avoid saying, "Read it and I will get back to you," This implies that a salesperson is "coming to get them." Remember, these are cold prospects, and we are shy. We don't want to press our luck.

Instead, we could say something like this, "Here, let me **loan** you this book. It is a short read. I can pick it up next week after you finish."

But what will compel prospects to call us after reading the book?

There is no legal restriction from us putting our personal advertising or message inside the back cover of the book. Our message could be as simple as, "I am using the principles in this book as step #1 of my two-step plan to retire in five years."

HOW TO GET APPOINTMENTS WITHOUT REJECTION

We can experiment with our messages. If we want to motivate people to call us, curiosity is a good tactic. It is not the only way, but it is a good way.

If we have good rapport when loaning the book, we could mention our promotional message then also. We don't have to make it a question. We only need to plant the seed for when they read the book.

This is an example of using a physical paperback book. Now, use our imagination. In a digital, virtual age, so many more possibilities exist.

However, remember this rule. A physical item carries more weight as a gift than a link on the Internet. It gives prospects the impression that we are sacrificing or making a bigger effort to help them.

Questions and objections.

Yes, they are the same thing.

Only interested prospects have questions and objections. Prospects who are not interested won't ask for additional information torture.

So if someone asks a question, or brings up an objection, good news! They may have a problem we can help with. If we look at this situation with empathy, the questions and objections are easy to answer. Let's do a few now.

Q. "How much will this cost me?"

A. "Sounds like you are tired of overpaying on your electricity bill. The best way to fix this is to get together to answer your questions, and see how much you are overpaying now. Let's set a time next week that works."

• • •

Q. "Can't you just send me a link to a website or video?"

A. "Sending you to 100 links of data is missing the big picture. I don't want to waste your time. First we should see if you and I are a good fit to work together. That is what is going to make the big difference."

• • •

Q. "Why can't you explain everything to me by text message?"

A. "First, my thumbs would get tired. But what we want to discuss first is if you and I can work together professionally. Let's chat for a few minutes by video."

• • •

Q. "Let me call you back, okay?"

A. "Great idea. Better yet, I will call you back. I don't want to leave that extra responsibility on you. I am sure you have enough things to keep track of during the week. Let me call you next Wednesday when it will be a better time for both of us."

• • •

Q. "Can you explain it to me over the phone now?"

A. "Sure. Here is the short story. Before you and I discuss a lot of business details, you and I should sit down, face-to-face, and see if we would enjoy working together. Make sense? New friends make the best business partners."

• • •

Q. "Will you try to sell me something?"

A. "I can show you what to do, but it is up to you to decide if you would like to do it."

• • •

Q. "Is this something I have to decide now?"

A. "I want to leave you with some choices for the future."

• • •

Q. "I don't have time for a part-time business."

A. "If you are like me, you will eventually get tired of commuting. I want to give you some options to think about for when that happens."

• • •

Q. "I am not sure I would be interested."

A. "You have some options now. Let me add one or two more."

• • •

Q. "I am happy with my current electricity supplier."

A. "When your next electricity bill comes, if you want it to be lower, I will show you what to do."

• • •

Q. "Can you and I simply meet, without my spouse?"

A. "We could, but I don't want to be rude. Husbands and wives are a team and have many different types of questions such as, 'How much time will this take from our family? Is this the direction we want to go now?' Let's all meet together at a conve-nient time."

• • •

Q. "Who is this again?"

A. "We met at the home exhibition on Friday, but we didn't get much chance to talk then. You were busy with all the booths you had to visit. But you filled out this card that asked me to call you. You wanted me to tell you how to get your future holidays at wholesale prices instead of the big retail prices they are charging your family now."

• • •

Q. "Who is this again?"

A. "We met at the Chamber of Commerce networking event. We wanted to talk more then, but there were so many people to meet. You gave me your card and asked me to call you later. You wanted to know how to get out of last month's speeding ticket court date."

• • •

Q. "I want to start a business for free. How much is this going to cost me?"

A. "The good news is you won't have to spend money for employees, a business telephone line, rent, and office space, or purchase a lot of insurance. A traditional business can cost you $500,000 or more to start. That is too much risk. However, you will have to make an investment in time, learning, and some initial supplies to get started. We don't want to be dreamers, but people that take action."

• • •

Q. "I am not interested in anything you offer!"

A. "I totally respect that. Makes sense. But could you do me a favor? I am looking for people who are currently dissatisfied with their careers, or want a big change. While this may not be for you, do you know anyone like that?"

• • •

Q. "How much will this cost me to change my utilities?"

A. "Relax. It costs nothing to change who sends you the bill. Of course you still have to pay your utility bills, but the good news is they will be smaller."

• • •

Q. "What are you selling?"

A. "Our company manufactures and sells all kinds of health products. But that is not what I want to talk to you about. I wanted to talk about the possibility of us partnering in a business relationship. Want to talk over lunch? The worst that can happen is we have good Italian food for lunch."

• • •

Q. "How long will this presentation last?"

A. "When we meet, you might take one look at my face and decide you don't want to be in business with me. I am okay with that. But hopefully you will give me 10 minutes to show you the big picture. Then we are done. If you'd like to discuss the possibilities further, then we can talk more. That is up to you."

• • •

Q. "I am too busy to meet. Why not just send me an email?"

A. "You are busy, but we both still have to eat lunch. Let's meet then."

• • •

Q. "Things are crazy here. I don't have time now."

A. "I totally understand. When is the least hectic time for you? Let's meet then."

• • •

Q. "I don't think I am interested now."

A. "Makes sense. I would like to leave you with some choices for the future."

Our prospects will have questions. We won't have all the answers, but we should at least have answers to the basic questions.

Summary.

The hardest part of setting appointments is our mindset. We tell ourselves a story of doom. If we can change our internal story, we win. Why?

Our internal story creates our intention and radiates our beliefs to prospects. When we truly want to help prospects, they know. Prospects react differently to people who want to help them.

This is the biggest challenge every networker faces. We get so excited about our benefits, we end up thinking too much about us and not enough about our prospects.

What about all the skills we learned in the last half of this book? Yes, they will make us sound a lot more professional. But this is the smaller challenge.

So what can we do immediately to improve our ability to get appointments?

Visit with satisfied customers. Listen to their stories of how much they appreciate the chance to take advantage of our products, or services, or opportunity. This doesn't take much effort.

And if we don't have any satisfied customers to talk to? No worries. There are many people in our organization who do. Satisfied customers are always happy to tell us their experiences.

Call someone now. Let's build our belief that what we have helps prospects.

Thank you.

Thank you for purchasing and reading this book. We hope you found some ideas that will work for you.

Before you go, would it be okay if we asked a small favor? Would you take just one minute and leave a sentence or two reviewing this book online? Your review can help others choose what they will read next. It would be greatly appreciated by many fellow readers.

Get 2 FREE Big Al Training Audios

Magic Words for Prospecting

Plus a Free eBook and the Big Al Newsletter!

BigAlBooks.com/free

Big Al Workshops and
Live Online Trainings

BigAlBooks.com/workshops

More from the Prospecting and Recruiting Series

Create Influence
10 Ways to Impress and Guide Others

How to Meet New People Guidebook
Overcome Fear and Connect Now

How to Get Your Prospect's Attention and Keep It!
Magic Phrases for Network Marketing

10 Shortcuts Into Our Prospects' Minds
Get network marketing decisions fast!

How To Prospect, Sell And Build Your Network Marketing Business With Stories

26 Instant Marketing Ideas To Build Your Network Marketing Business

51 Ways and Places to Sponsor New Distributors
Discover Hot Prospects For Your Network Marketing Business

First Sentences for Network Marketing
How To Quickly Get Prospects On Your Side

Big Al's MLM Sponsoring Magic
How To Build A Network Marketing Team Quickly

Start SuperNetworking!
5 Simple Steps to Creating Your Own Personal Networking Group

More Books from Big Al Books
BigAlBooks.com

Getting Started Series

How to Build Your Network Marketing Business in 15 Minutes a Day

3 Easy Habits For Network Marketing
Automate Your MLM Success

Quick Start Guide for Network Marketing
Get Started FAST, Rejection-FREE!

Core Skills Series

How To Get Instant Trust, Belief, Influence and Rapport!
13 Ways To Create Open Minds By Talking To The
Subconscious Mind

Ice Breakers!
How To Get Any Prospect To Beg You For A Presentation

Pre-Closing for Network Marketing
"Yes" Decisions Before The Presentation

The Two-Minute Story for Network Marketing
Create the Big-Picture Story That Sticks!

Personality Training Series (The Colors)

The Four Color Personalities for MLM
The Secret Language for Network Marketing

Mini-Scripts for the Four Color Personalities
How to Talk to our Network Marketing Prospects

Why Are My Goals Not Working?
Color Personalities for Network Marketing Success

How To Get Kids To Say Yes!
Using the Secret Four Color Languages to Get Kids to Listen

Presentation and Closing Series

Closing for Network Marketing
Getting Prospects Across The Finish Line

The One-Minute Presentation
Explain Your Network Marketing Business Like A Pro

How to Follow Up With Your Network Marketing Prospects
Turn Not Now Into Right Now!

Retail Sales for Network Marketers
How to Get New Customers for Your MLM Business

Leadership Series

The Complete Three-Book Network Marketing Leadership Series
Series includes: How To Build Network Marketing Leaders Volume One, How To Build Network Marketing Leaders Volume Two, and Motivation. Action. Results.

How To Build Network Marketing Leaders
Volume One: Step-By-Step Creation Of MLM Professionals

How To Build Network Marketing Leaders
Volume Two: Activities And Lessons For MLM Leaders

Motivation. Action. Results.
How Network Marketing Leaders Move Their Teams

More Books...

Why You Need to Start Network Marketing
How to Remove Risk and Have a Better Life

How To Build Your Network Marketing Nutrition Business Fast

How Speakers, Trainers, and Coaches Get More Bookings
12 Ways to Flood Our Calendars with Paid Events

How To Build Your Network Marketing Utilities Business Fast

Getting "Yes" Decisions
What insurance agents and financial advisors can say to clients

Public Speaking Magic
Success and Confidence in the First 20 Seconds

Worthless Sponsor Jokes
Network Marketing Humor

About the Authors

Keith Schreiter has 20+ years of experience in network marketing and MLM. He shows network marketers how to use simple systems to build a stable and growing business.

So, do you need more prospects? Do you need your prospects to commit instead of stalling? Want to know how to engage and keep your group active? If these are the types of skills you would like to master, you will enjoy his "how-to" style.

Keith speaks and trains in the U.S., Canada, and Europe.

Tom "Big Al" Schreiter has 40+ years of experience in network marketing and MLM. As the author of the original "Big Al" training books in the late '70s, he has continued to speak in over 80 countries on using the exact words and phrases to get prospects to open up their minds and say "YES."

His passion is marketing ideas, marketing campaigns, and how to speak to the subconscious mind in simplified, practical ways. He is always looking for case studies of incredible marketing campaigns that give usable lessons.

As the author of numerous audio trainings, Tom is a favorite speaker at company conventions and regional events.

Printed in Poland
by Amazon Fulfillment
Poland Sp. z o.o., Wrocław

61985576R00067

Fear? Sweaty palms? Don't know what to say? Afraid of how others will react?

Why do we avoid setting appointments? Our self-image says to us, "Don't take a chance."

Motivation alone won't fix this. Our minds will come up with excuses not to set the appointment.

Our sponsor yells at us, "Face the fear, and the fear will go away." Sounds easy to say, but to do? Not as easy.

Appointments are part of our business. We must fix this problem. We will have to make setting appointments enjoyable. Then, our brains will work for us instead of against us.

How can we make setting appointments enjoyable? First, we will learn to make appointments a passion, something we look forward to. And second? We will learn the exact words to say to avoid rejection and to reduce tension with our prospects.

Tom "Big Al" Schreiter

Keith Schreiter

Let's face it. No one wants to be a pushy salesperson. We want to be a welcome addition to other people's lives. We can do this by following certain principles such as being brief, getting to the point, making it all about our prospects, and presenting our offer as a way of improving their lives.

No more fear. No more feeling guilty. Instead, let's turn our negative feelings into positive momentum to get appointments fast. We want to enjoy every moment of our business.

BIG AL SERIES

PROSPECTING AND **RECRUITING**

BigAlBooks.com/prospecting

$12.95
ISBN-13: 978-1-948197-71-7

ISBN 9781948197717

90000